Single Parent Dating

The Guide for Building a Healthy and Lasting Relationship as a Single Parent

By Cynthia Cherry

Foreword

Raising a child (or children) is very rewarding but it is also quite challenging – especially if you find yourself doing it alone. Being a single parent is never easy – you must put your children first which often means that some of your own needs may go unmet. There comes a point, however, when you realize that you no longer need to (or want to) do it on your own – a time when you are ready to start dating again. But how do you do about re-entering the dating scene as a single parent who has been off the market for years, or even decades? It is not easy!

Single parent dating is incredibly challenging it its own way but the challenge is worth the effort if you end up with a loving partner in the end. In this book you will learn everything you need to know about single parent dating including steps to take before you enter the dating scene and recommendations for what to do when you are ready to start dating again. By the time you finish this book you will know for sure whether or not you are ready to start dating again and, if you are, you will have a roadmap to guide you through the process.

Foreword

Table of Contents

Introduction

New relationships can be exciting, but they also come with challenges, especially when children are involved. As a single parent, you are not alone when you start dating – you must consider the effect on your children every step of the way. There is never a perfect time to start dating again but moving on is a necessary part of life so you should be prepared to do it eventually. But how do you know when you are ready and where do you start?

In this book you will receive a detailed guide for navigating the world of dating as a single parent. Here you will find tips for questions to ask yourself as you think about putting yourself out there and, when you are ready to start dating again, you'll find helpful information about where to start your search for that special someone. Within the pages of this book you will find a wealth of information for everything from first date ideas to tips for figuring out the sexual aspects of a new relationship.

There is no blueprint for dating as a single parent – each situation is unique because you and your children are unique. But if you are careful and thoughtful you will find that the transition back into the dating world comes a little easier and that any negative effects on your children can be minimized. There may not be any "right" way to start dating again, but the information in this guide book will help you to avoid the "wrongs".

If you are thinking about starting to date again as a single parent, turn the page and start learning!

Chapter One: Are You Ready to Start Dating Again?

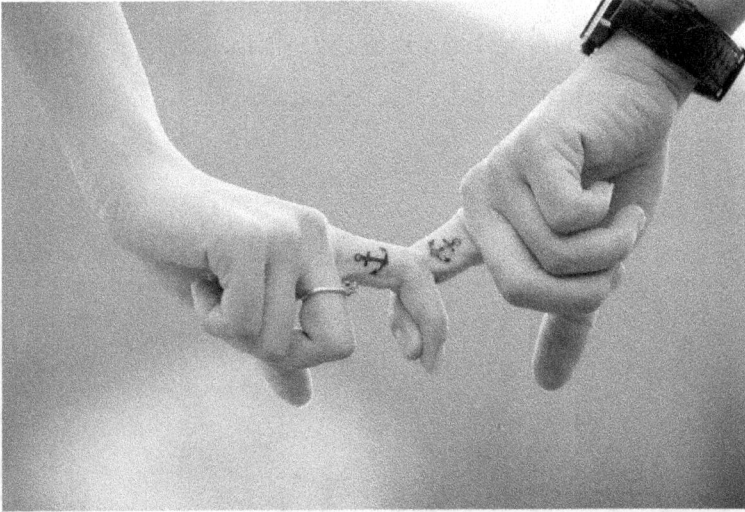

According to a 2009 report released by the U.S. Census Bureau, there are more than 13.7 million single parents in the United States and they are raising a total of 22 million children. Those 22 million children represent about a quarter of the children under 21 that are living in the United States today. These numbers show that while you may at times feel like you are alone as a single parent, you really aren't. There are millions more like you who struggle with the same things you do on a daily basis! Being a single parent is just like anything else – you eventually learn how to deal with it. But just because you have gotten the hang of single parenting doesn't mean you have to stay single forever! In this chapter, you will find some important questions to ask yourself if you are thinking about getting back into the dating scene. Asking yourself these questions ahead of time will help you enter the dating pool in a healthy and practical state of mind.

1.) Dating for the Right Reasons

As a parent, single or not, most of your life revolves around your kids. But for many single parents, when the children get old enough that they can enjoy some level of independence, it is the perfect time to start dating again. Before you put yourself out there, however, you should take the time to think carefully about why you want to start dating again. <u>Ask yourself the following questions</u>:

- Are you looking for someone to share the load of caring for/raising your kids?

- Are you looking for an opportunity to have a no-strings-attached fling with someone?

- Are you bored and looking for an excuse to get out of the house without the kids?

If you answered "yes" to any of these questions you should probably take a step back and examine your motives. You may also want to think about your particular situation – what caused you to become a single parent. Are you separated from your partner or did you get divorced? Have you been widowed? Did your partner abandon you and your children? Your relationship background will play an important role in determining how soon you will be ready to start dating again and what your motivations for doing so might be.

Dating as a single parent isn't as breezy and carefree as dating as a teenager or young adult – you are not the only one who will be affected by your new relationship. It is important that you approach single parent dating from a practical perspective in order to protect yourself and your children in a new relationship. <u>On the next page, you will find a list of some of the healthier, practical reasons single parents start dating again</u>:

- You are satisfied with your life but you feel like it could be improved by sharing it with someone else.

- You are lonely and longing to make a strong connection with someone like-minded.

- You want to share your life and your children with someone special so the two of you can grow old together.

- You want to get married again sometime in the future or you want to have more children.

- You long for an intimate connection with someone, both physical and emotional.

As you start to think about your reasons to get back into the dating scene you may find that you are anxious about connecting with other single parents. After all, it is hard enough to raise a child (or children) on your own, so dating someone who is also a single parent could get complicated. <u>Before you get discouraged, however, consider these eight reasons to date a single parent</u>:

1. Single parents are strong and independent – they already have a handle on their own lives and they don't play silly games.

2. A single parent already knows how to be a good parent – this is important because you want to find someone who will bond with your child. You may also be looking to have more children in the future.

3. You won't find yourself waiting around and guessing how they feel about you – dating as a single parent isn't a solitary thing, you always must keep your children in mind. If the relationship isn't right, you'll know.

4. Single parents are incredibly loyal and dedicated to family – they have to be in order to succeed in raising a child (or children) alone.

5. A single parent is selfless – they are always putting others (particularly their children) before themselves.

6. As a single parent, you have had to adapt to unexpected changes and challenging situations – other single parents have this experience as well so the two of you won't be torn apart by bumps in the road.

7. Single parents tend not to rush into things because they have to always do what's best for their kids – this means that you will be able to take the relationship as slowly as you need to.

8. Most single parents take dating very seriously and they know what they want – they won't waste their time if they don't feel like something is right.

Now that you've thought about why you want to start dating again it is time to move on to the next question – do you have time to start dating?

2.) Do You Have the Time?

We all lead busy and hectic lives but many of us have the benefit of a supportive partner or spouse. For single parents, the challenge of raising a child and running a household becomes even more difficult because you are doing it on your own. Your days are filled with making lunches, driving carpools, attending PTA meetings, and more – and all of that is on top of your own job and your own life! Before you start dating again, you should seriously ask yourself whether you have the time to devote to starting a new relationship.

Everyone has their own dating style, so you may not need to have a lot of spare time to devote to dating in the beginning. You may want to start off slow with a few telephone conversations, maybe one lunch or dinner date during the week. As your new relationship starts to grow stronger, you can find ways to work some additional time together into your schedule. It may be challenging, but if you are serious about getting back into the dating scene you will find time to make it happen. Just be sure that your new relationship doesn't take up any time with your kids – they are still the most important thing in your life.

3.) What are You Looking For?

Once you've determined that you are ready to start dating again and that you have the time to do so, you need to think about what you are looking for. Keep in mind that this may change over the course of a relationship. For example, you may start out with the desire to meet new people and to make new friends. As those friendships develop, however, you may find that your desires change and you start to want a romantic connection rather than a platonic one. Just be open and honest with yourself (and your partner) about what you have to give and what you want from the relationship.

Not only do you need to think about what kind of relationship you are looking for, but you should also think about what kind of partner you want. While physical traits are important for fostering a chemical bond between you and your new partner, you also need to think about the personality traits and characteristics that you value most. Here are some additional questions to ask yourself to help you decide what you want in a partner:

- Does this person share many of your values and opinions?
- Does this person have an interest in the things that you enjoy?
- Is this person open and honest about their feelings?
- Is this person loyal to friends and family?
- Does this person treat you with respect and honor your boundaries?
- Does this person support you in your accomplishments as well as your failures?

- Is this person someone that you can talk to easily, even about difficult subjects?
- Is this person the kind of parent and person you want your children to be exposed to?
- Does this person want the same thing from a relationship as you?
- Does this person trust you and make themselves worthy of your trust?
- Is this person respectful of your time, understanding that your children come first?
- Is this person someone who makes you feel good about yourself and in general?

These are just a few of the many questions you should be asking yourself before you enter the dating pool and once you start meeting new people. It is important that you keep a clear head and an open mind throughout the entire process for your own sake as well as the sake of your children.

Chapter Two: Where Should You Look?

Now that you've thought about why you want to start dating and what you are looking for in a new partner, you may be wondering how you go about finding your special someone. While you can meet people just about anywhere (even at the grocery store!), you may not want to leave things up to chance. If you know what you are ready to start dating, you should be intentional about giving yourself opportunities to meet new people and, when you do, you should start off as friends. In this chapter, you will learn about the importance of shared interests in choosing a mate and receive tips for starting a new relationship.

1.) How Important Are Similar Interests?

If you have been out of the dating scene for a while, you may feel like you have no idea where to start. Depending how your last relationship ended, you may even feel like the things you want in a mate have changed as well. No matter what you are looking for a in a new partner, however, it is always a good idea to start by looking for someone who shares some of your interests, hobbies, and passions. You don't want to pair up with someone who is exactly like you, but having shared interests will give you things to talk about and an easy way to make that initial connection. Just because you have shared interests doesn't necessarily mean that the two of you will be compatible, but it certainly doesn't hurt.

Having shared interests gives you and your new partner a foundation on which to build your relationship. Not only will it give you something to talk about during that awkward first date, but it also means that the two of you have some activities you can enjoy doing together. Not only is it beneficial to have shared interests with your new partner, but having shared values an also play a major role in strengthening your relationship. In fact, many relationship experts say that shared values are more important than shared interests for a couple.

Though there are many who believe that shared interests are a great foundation for a new relationship, there are just as many who disagree. <u>Here are some of the reasons why a relationship founded on shared interests may not work out</u>:

- Conversations can become repetitive or they may not be interesting if you both have the same opinions.
- If you and your partner align on most issues, you may not challenge each other to become a stronger or a better person.
- Too many shared interests could lead to complacency – you may not be adventurous or spontaneous in the relationship.

- You may grow tired of the person you are with or you may feel like you are dating another version of yourself.

There is no "yes" or "no" answer to the question of how important is it to have shared interests with your partner because each relationship is different. In the end, you really need to find what is right for you and follow your heart. You should also think about starting off as friends with your new partner – you will learn more about that in the next section.

2.) Starting Off as Friends

As a single parent, everything you do affects your kids in some way. This being the case, you need to be very careful when you start dating – you don't want things to move too quickly. Many agree that the best way to keep a new relationship from moving too fast is to start out as friends. But is it possible for men and women to have a platonic friendship? The results of a study conducted by the University of Texas at Austin and Northwestern University suggest that not only is it possible, but it gives your relationship a higher chance of long-term success.

This study involved a total of 167 dating and married couples. Researchers asked the couples how long they had known each other and how long they had been romantically involved. The results showed that 40% of couples were friends before they started dating and 41% were not – the remaining 20% either didn't respond or gave different answers from their partners. Another interesting part of this study was that researchers rated each individual on his or her objective attractiveness.

The primary finding of the study was that couples who were friends prior to dating were more likely to have a larger attractiveness gap (one partner was significantly more attractive than the other). But what does this mean? Yes, it does point out that, as humans, we can be shallow beings, but it also means that relationships founded on an emotional connection rather than a physical one tend to last longer. The more you and your partner understand each other, the stronger your relationship will be. If you rush into a sexual relationship too quickly, you could skip that step.

Though there is a great deal of support for the idea that being friends with your partner first will lead to a stronger relationship, there are also those who believe the opposite. Paul Dobransky, a blogger for Psychology Today and the co-author of *The Secret Psychology of How We Fall in Love*, suggests that any successful relationship goes through three phases and friendship comes in second. The first phase of any relationship, according to Dobransky, is attraction – there must be something about the other person that draws you to them – it doesn't always have to be physical. After that initial attraction comes friendship and that leads eventually to commitment.

3.) Should You Consider Online Dating?

If you haven't heard of online dating sites like eHarmony and Match.com then you must live under a rock. These and other dating websites have become the new modern way to meet people and they offer some excellent benefits for single parents. For one thing, dating online means that you don't have to find the time to get dressed up and leave your house in hopes of meeting someone. Not only can you start online dating from home, but you can do it in the comfort of your PJs, if you want to!

Not only is online dating easy and convenient, but it gives you access to hundreds, even thousands, of eligible singles whom you might never have a chance to meet otherwise. Online dating allows you to search for potential partners based on whatever criteria you value most – certain physical traits, education level, age, income, lifestyle, values, interests, and more. This allows you to weed out all of the people you know you won't be compatible with so you can start connecting with potential matches right away. The biggest challenge with online dating is choosing who to connect with – you have so many options!

Another important benefit of online dating is that it is a safe and low-key way to meet new people. Online, a relationship can start with something as simple as a one-word message and it gives you the opportunity to communicate with your potential partner in a low-stress environment. It also allows you to take things as fast or as slow as you like. Many single parents meet people online then talk to them on the phone before meeting them in person. You have complete control over how your relationship progresses.

If you think that online dating might be a good option for you, here is a list of some of the top dating websites that are geared specifically toward single parents:

- SingleParentLove.com
- SingleParentMeet.com
- SingleParentsMingle.com
- SingleMomsAndDads.com

- SingleParentsMatcher.com

When it comes to meeting new people, online dating isn't the only option. Many single parents end up meeting people at the gym, for example. If you value physical fitness and a healthy lifestyle, meeting someone at a gym means that they probably share some of your values and interests. You can also find single parents at local events like concerts, shows, and fundraisers. If you have young children, you may be able to connect with other single parents at the park or at other places you take your children.

Chapter Three: First Date Ideas

Once you have found someone you feel a connection with, the next step is to start dating! But how do you make the leap from talking to dating and what should you do for your first date? If it's been a while since you were in the dating pool, questions like these can seem overwhelming. In this chapter, you will learn about the do's and don'ts of first dates. You will also receive some tips for having a date at a restaurant as well as some conversation starters. With all of this information in mind you can enter the dating pool again with confidence and a positive attitude.

1.) Where NOT to Have a First Date

Before you start thinking about where to have your first date with a new love interest, you should be aware of certain things that do NOT make good first dates. Choosing the right location for your first date is incredibly important because this is the first time that the two of you will be spending any real time together. You want to choose an activity you both enjoy, but you also want to make sure that anything you choose gives you two a chance to talk and get to know one another.

On the following page, you will find a few things that do NOT make good first dates:

- **Going to a movie**. A first date is probably not the best opportunity to see that new movie you've been dying to see. You might enjoy the movie, but you won't be able to talk to your date and you'll end the night in the same place you started – knowing nothing about each other.

- **Going to a restaurant**. A dinner date is the go-to for many people when it comes to first dates but there are many reasons why this may not be the best option. For one thing, it forces the two of you to spend the evening staring at each other, peppering the other with questions. Dinner dates can get very personal very quickly and it can be an awkward situation for the both of you.

- **Going to a family function**. Inviting your date to a family picnic may sound like a fun, care-free date but it can actually be very stressful and intimidating for your date. Introducing a new partner to the family on the first date is too much too soon.

- **Going on a group activity**. Inviting your new love interest to join you on a group outing with your friends might also seem like a good date idea but, again, it puts a lot of pressure on your date and you may not have the chance to really get to know each other with all of those extra people around.

- **Hanging out at home**. It may seem like a good idea to have a casual date at home as your first meeting, but it generally isn't. Inviting your date to "hang out" shows that you don't have enough interest in them to plan something and it could send the wrong signals about your intentions.

- **Going to the mall**. Having a first date at the mall may seem like a good chance to spend some time together and shopping will give you something to talk about. But, in many cases, this kind of date backfires because it is an impersonal activity.

There are many more activities that make for bad first dates but, by now, you should have an understanding of what makes a bad date bad. If the date doesn't give you an opportunity to spend some face-to-face time with your date and if it doesn't allow you to talk and get to know each other, it's probably not a good first date. First dates should be fun, so engaging in some kind of activity is always good, as long as it doesn't prevent you from really connecting and talking to each other.

2.) *Fun, Friendly and Free Date Ideas*

Now that you know what makes for a bad first date, you may be wondering about what makes for a good first date. First dates are always a little bit stressful, but planning ahead can take some of the pressure off. For example, it never hurts to have some topics for conversation prepared – don't memorize a monologue, but think of some funny stories you can tell or questions you want to ask your date. An ideal first date will leave opportunities for conversation while also allowing you and your date to have some fun together with a shared interest or activity.

While you and your date are enjoying some time together, try to keep things light and casual as much as possible. If an awkward moment occurs, don't sit there sweating – make a joke about it to diffuse the tension. If things are going well between you, don't be afraid to initiate a little bit of physical contact to show your date that you are interested – a hand on the shoulder or a touch to the arm can communicate your feelings without words.

To help you decide what to do on your first date, here are some simple date ideas that are fun, friendly, and free:

- **Go for a hike in a local park**. Going for a hike is a simple but enjoyable activity that also leaves plenty of time for you two to talk and get to know each other.

- **Find a free concert in your area**. Free concerts are the perfect summer date and they give you an activity to plan around starting with dinner and ending with post-concert drinks.

- **Visit your local farmers' market**. Going to a farmers' market or a food festival can be fun and you'll be able to snack on free samples!

- **Go to a museum that offers free admission**. Find out what kind of interests your date has and then pick a museum you can both enjoy like an art museum, a museum of natural history, or a local history museum.

- **Attend a trivia night**. Find a local bar that offers trivia night and pair up together to see how well you do. You may impress your date with your knowledge or you may end up laughing about how horrible you are at trivia.

- **Visit some local art galleries**. Look up some local art galleries and make an afternoon (or evening) crawl out of it. Many cities actually sponsor art crawls where the galleries offer refreshments.

- **Go on a brewery tour**. Many brewery tours are free and, best of all, you'll get free beer samples! You may also be able to find distillery or winery tours in your area.

- **Have a game night**. Take some of your favorite childhood board games to a coffee shop and spend the evening playing Chutes and Ladders and Candyland.

- **Go to the beach**. If the weather is nice and warm, a beach date is a great idea! Take a picnic with you and spend some time relaxing by the water.

- **Volunteer somewhere together**. From serving meals at a homeless shelter to walking rescue dogs, there are countless opportunities for volunteering in your area and it can make for a great first date.

- **Go for a scenic drive**. Hop in the car and hit the road, exploring a new area of the city that you've never been to or take advantage of back roads.

- **Make a scavenger hunt**. Together, create a list of items you might find then take your list with you as you explore a new part of town, looking for the items on your list.

Another great way to come up with free date ideas is to check your local newspaper. Most city papers have a section where they advertise local events – this is a great place to look for date ideas.

3.) Tips for First Dates at a Restaurant

Although there are certain things about having a first date at a restaurant that are not ideal, there are ways you can make this kind of date work. Below you will find some simple tips for making your first dinner date a success:

- **Choose a restaurant you've been to before**. Selecting a restaurant that neither of you has ever been to will just add to the stress of the date – you want to enter your date with confidence, so picking a place you've been to before will help with that. Plus, if you've been to the restaurant before you know that the food is good and you may even be able to make recommendations to your date.

- **Don't choose a restaurant that is TOO familiar**. You want to choose a restaurant that you've been to before, but don't pick your local watering hole where the bartender and the wait staff know you by name. It may seem like a good way to impress your date but they will probably just end up wondering how often you bring dates there.

- **Make it seem like a special occasion**. Don't just pick a restaurant that is a block from your house – you want the date to become an event so that your date feels special. Plus, telling your date that you live a block away may give them the wrong idea about your intentions.

- **Ask your date about preferences**. Nothing is worse than planning a first date at a steak house just to find that your date is a vegetarian. It never hurts to ask if your date has any food allergies or preferences to make sure that you can find a restaurant that works for both of you.

- **Don't choose the most expensive restaurant**. Taking your date to a fancy restaurant may seem like a way to make a good first impression, but the price may make some people unconformable. You want to be able to focus on getting to know your date instead of worrying about whether you're using the right fork.

- **Don't make assumptions about the check**. While it may be tradition for the man to pick up the check (especially if he initiated the date), but that doesn't mean you should sit by and expect your date to pay. Offer to pay your half of the bill and make sure you have enough cash to cover it, just in case.

- **Always tip appropriately**. The amount a person tips says a lot about them – it shows whether they are generous or stingy. You can always offer to leave the tip yourself if your date picks up the check.

- **Go where the night takes you**. If your dinner date goes well, you should have a plan for how to keep the night going – maybe you know a bowling alley nearby or a coffee shop that is open late. Having a contingency plan will help to reduce your anxiety and it will make a good impression on your date!

4.) Conversation Starters and Tips

Actually deciding what you are going to do for your first date is difficult enough, but you also need to think about what you two are going to talk about. Awkward silences are bound to happen, but thinking ahead about some topics of conversation can help you to navigate the awkwardness. Don't memorize a monologue to recite for your date, but be ready with some conversation starters like those listed here below:

- What accomplishment are you most proud of?
- What is your favorite book or movie and why?
- If you could take a vacation anywhere in the world, where would you go?

- If you could change one thing about your job, what would it be?
- What was the worst date you have ever been on?
- If you suddenly had a million dollars, what would you do first?
- What is your "guilty pleasure" television show?
- Is there a strange food combination that you love?
- What do you like to do in your spare time?
- If you could magically acquire a certain talent or skill, what would it be?
- What kind of music do you like to listen to?
- What do you usually do on the weekend?
- Have you been on a vacation lately? If so, where?
- What is your favorite childhood memory?
- Who is the most influential person in your life?
- If you had to choose one weapon during a zombie apocalypse, what would it be?
- If you had three wishes, what would you wish for?
- What is the strangest or worst job you've ever had?
- What is your favorite (or least favorite) pickup line?

The questions above offer some simple ways to start a conversation with your date while still keeping things fairly light-hearted. According to a recent study, if you really want to make a good impression on your date (and increase the chances for a second date), there are certain topics that you should hit. Travel is a great topic for first dates and sharing a secret or other emotional/personal information is the best way to form a connection during the first date. Even talking about controversial topics can lead to a deeper connection with your date than "safe" topics.

Chapter Four: When Should You Get Your Kids Involved?

As a single parent, you must always consider your children in everything that you do. When you start dating again, you need to think not just about how this new relationship will affect you, but also how it could impact your children. While you should think about these things in theory, you shouldn't actually introduce your children to your new partner until everyone is ready. In this chapter, you'll receive some helpful information about how a new relationship could affect your kids and you will receive some tips for how to tell your children about your new partner and how to make the introductions.

1.) How Does a New Relationship Affect Your Kids?

When you find that special someone it is easy to get caught up in the excitement. But as a single parent, everything you do has an effect on your children and you need to be aware of that. At some point, if you and your partner see a future together, you will need to get your kids involved but it is important that you do not rush this step. In the same way that you needed time to get over your last relationship before dating again, your children need time to adjust to the changes that resulted from the end of that relationship before they can accept your new partner.

Before you even think about introducing your kids to your new partner, you should think about the effect that your new relationship could have on your kids. When a child loses a parent (either to divorce or death), it can be extremely traumatizing. If your previous partner died, your child will go through a period of mourning – some children take longer than others to come to terms with this loss. If your relationship ended in divorce or abandonment, it can actually be even more difficult for your child to reconcile with the idea that your family will never be the same.

Introducing your children to your new partner can also bring up feelings of divided loyalty. Some children feel like if they accept their new stepparent it means that they are giving up on their natural parent. If your previous partner is still involved, it could be difficult for your child to get used to having a stepparent in addition to two real parents. It may be especially difficult for your child to cope if your new partner plays a role in enforcing rules in the household or in dealing out discipline. You and your partner will need to talk about how you will slowly start to blend your families to make sure that the transition is as smooth as possible for both of your children.

2.) *The Dangers of Involving Kids too Early*

By now it's been said a million times, but when you are a single parent your life is not completely your own – every decision you make and every action you take has an impact on your children. When you find that special someone that you want to spend your life with, you need to make sure that they are going to get along with your kids before you take the next step. But there are some dangers involved with introducing your new partner to your kids too soon. <u>Here are some examples</u>:

- If you introduce your kids to your new partner too early (before you and your partner talk about the future), it could be confusing for your kids because your partner doesn't have a specific role.

- If you introduce your new partner to your kids and they become attached, it could be devastating for your kids if the two of you split.

- If you introduce your partner to your kids before they have reconciled with the end of your previous relationship, they may have hard feelings toward your new partner.

- If you allow your new partner to take on a role in your children's lives before they are ready, they could act out or become bitter toward your partner.

Many experts agree that you should date your new partner for at least a year before you introduce your children. While this is a good rule of thumb to keep in mind, it is not a hard and fast rule that applies to every situation. For example, if your previous partner died, it may take longer for your children to cope with the loss than if your partner were still involved in their lives. At the same time, however, introducing a new partner before the relationship is officially over can also be confusing. Your best bet is to move slowly and to talk to your partner before you take any new steps.

3.) Tips for Getting Your Kids Involved

If you think that the time is right to introduce your new partner to your children, there are some simple Dos and Don'ts you should follow. For one thing, you need to be aware of your child's current state of mind so you can predict potential questions or problems. Is your child still mourning the loss of a parent? Is their performance in school suffering? Are there other factors causing stress for your child? How long has it been since your prior relationship ended? Asking yourself these questions can help you to determine whether the time is right to bring your new partner into the picture.

In addition to thinking about how your children will respond, you also need to know whether or not your new partner is ready to meet. You and your new partner need to be secure in your relationship before you even think about bringing your kids into the question. You need to think about your motives and your goals for this relationship – are you looking for a new life partner or just someone to have fun with? Do you see a future with this person or are you not really that serious yet? You need to make sure that everyone involved is ready for the introduction.

When it comes to making the actual introduction between your kids and your new partner, here are some tips:

- If your previous partner is still involved, let them know that you will be introducing your kids to your new partner – give your ex the chance to meet your new partner first, if so desired.

- Plan for a short introductory meeting – somewhere between 30 and 60 minutes is about as long as this first meeting should be.

- Choose a casual location and activity for your first meeting – a sleepover might not be a good idea but grabbing some ice cream or going to the park are all good options.

- Introduce your new partner to your kids and let your kids ask some questions, if they have them, or give them a chance to tell your partner a little about themselves.

- Gradually increase the length of your meetings, slowly giving your partner and your kids more time together.

While it can be tempting to just throw everyone together and hope for the best, making introductions between your kids and your new partner is not something you should rush. As you all start spending more time together, keep an eye on how your kids are adjusting and address any questions or concerns as soon as they arise. Over time, your kids will hopefully get used to your new partner and vice versa.

Chapter Five: Sex in a New Relationship

Intimacy is an important part of any relationship – single parents included - but when there are children involved it is important to make sure that things don't move too quickly in your new relationship. You also want to make sure that you and your new partner have established an emotional bond – that you develop some level of compatibility before you start addressing issues of sexuality. In this chapter, you will learn about the effects of introducing sex into a new relationship too soon and you will receive tips for talking to your kids about it.

1.) How Soon is Too Soon?

Many single parents want to know an exact number for how many weeks or months they should wait before having sex with a new partner. Taking this kind of step in your new relationship is huge and once you take it, you can't take it back, so it is not something you want to rush into. Research shows that most couples have their first kiss by the time of their second date, but humans on average wait 4 to 6 dates before having sex, and we wait an average of 14 dates before saying "I love you". But every couple is unique so you need to make this decision on your own instead of following some kind of formula.

According to a 2010 study conducted by Dean Busby, the director of the school of family life at Brigham Young University, the longer you wait to have sex, the more satisfying and stable your relationship will be – especially if you wait until marriage. To give you another perspective, Toni Coleman, a psychotherapist, suggests that waiting three months (until the honeymoon phase is over) is the best time to for a couple to start having sex. Waiting about three months is enough time to develop an emotional as well as a physical connection with your partner.

In the end, it is really up to you and your partner to decide when it is right to start having sex. For some people, physical chemistry is closely related to emotional closeness while others prefer to really wait and get to know their partner before becoming intimate. The best thing you can do is to be open and honest with your partner – have a conversation about it! This is the best way to make sure that you don't have sex too soon in a relationship and that you don't wait so long that your sexual chemistry with the other person subsides.

2.) When are Sleepovers Okay?

In addition to thinking carefully about when you and your new partner are ready to have sex, you need to think about when it is and is not okay to have sleepovers. As a single parent, most of your evenings are probably consumed by dinner prep, homework, and bedtime stories. Finding the time to schedule a sleepover can be tricky, especially if you want to wait until your kids are out of the house. If your ex is not in the picture, however, this could be a very rare occasion. You will need to think about whether it is okay for your child to know that your partner is sleeping over.

Many single parents agree that you should not engage in sleepovers until your children have met your new partner and they are comfortable having him or her around. Not only should you and your new partner spend time with your kids outside the home, but your kids should also get used to your new partner being around the house. Invite your partner over for dinners and family movie nights – anything to get your kids using to having your new partner around so that when he or she is there when your kids wake up, it won't be a problem.

In addition to making sure that your kids are used to your new partner being around the house, you should also have a conversation with your kids (if they are old enough) about letting your partner sleep over. This can be a challenge for a number of different reasons. For older children, having your partner sleep over may raise questions about why your child can't have his or her significant other sleep over. The best thing to do here is to explain to your child that when they are an adult, they can make their own decisions in their own home. But for now, your rules must be followed in your house – and that should be the end of it.

For younger children, initiating sleepovers can be a little more challenging when it comes to making the transition. For younger children, your best bet is to make sure that their nighttime routine isn't interrupted. You and your child probably have a routine for taking a bath, brushing teeth, and getting tucked into bed. As long as you keep up with that routine, your child may not even notice that your partner is sleeping over. If your child is young, he or she may not understand what an adults-only sleepover means, but that doesn't mean you should actively hide it from them. The best course of action may be to simply say to your child, "Do you remember so and so? They are going to sleep over tonight so they might be here when we have breakfast in the morning".

3.) How do You Talk to Your Kids?

When your new partner starts to sleep over at your house, or vice versa, it could bring up questions about sex for your kids. This may mean that you end up talking to your child about the "birds and the bees" earlier than you planned to, but it is better to do so earlier rather than later. One thing you want to make sure your children understand is that sex is a meaningful connection between two people – it is an act of love and not an action that should be taken thoughtlessly. If your kids are too young to understand anything else about sex, that is an important lesson for them to learn.

If your kids are old enough to have an intelligent conversation about sex, you need to be careful about how you approach the issue. Do not use the conversation as an opportunity to scare your child, telling them horror stories about STDs. Take the opportunity to dispel any myths and rumors your child may have heard and give them a chance to ask questions. You can also ask them questions about what their friends have told them or what they have experienced as a means of educating your child further. Just don't press too hard with the questions because it could cause your child to close up.

Chapter Six: Quick Tips for Single Parent Dating

At this point you should have a thorough understanding of the challenges and benefits of single parent dating. You must remember as you move forward that each situation is different – you may approach dating differently than another single parent might – so you need to find what works for you. Most single parents find that going slow is the best way to ensure that dating doesn't interfere with parenting duties and to make sure that it is healthy and fulfilling for both parties. To help you succeed in finding a new partner and starting a new relationship, keep these top ten single parent dating tips in mind:

1. Think carefully before you start dating again to make sure that it is the right move for you and your children – don't start dating again too quickly after your marriage (or relationship) ends.

2. Remember that you are doing more than just starting a relationship – you are building a family. You are not alone when you start dating!

3. Think long and hard about yourself and your needs before you start thinking about someone else. Why do you want to start dating again and what are you really looking for?

4. Talk to your children about the possibility of you dating again (if they are old enough) – give your kids a chance to ask questions and be open with them all the way through.

5. Think about when and how you will introduce your children to your new partner and discuss it with him/her. When you are ready to make introductions, make sure that your kids are ready as well.

6. Address any issues that your children have right away – acknowledge any fears and give your kids the chance to talk about their concerns.

7. Move slowly with your new relationship and make sure to keep a balance between your home life with your kids and your new dating life. New relationships can be exciting but don't let your relationship with your kids suffer.

8. Don't force your kids to spend time with your partner and don't be upset if they don't like them right away – everyone will need time to adjust to a new situation.

9. Remember that a strong relationship is built on more than just a physical bond – be honest with yourself about your new partner's character and flaws when considering whether they are the right person for you and your family.

10. Learn as much as you can about blended families – a family that includes step-children and step-parents comes with its own unique set of challenges that you should be prepared for.

These are just a few of the many things you can think about or do to make sure that your new relationship goes well and that your dating life doesn't have a negative effect on your kids.

Chapter Seven: When Should You Mention the "M" Word?

When it comes to dating, marriage is the ultimate goal for many people, though not for all. As a single parent, you may find yourself dealing with some unique challenges. Entering into a new marriage as a single parent is tricky, especially if both of you already have children. In this chapter you will receive some helpful tips for determining the right time to start thinking about marriage as well as recommendations for how to involve your children in the decision. You'll also receive tips for navigating the challenges of having a blended family.

1.) When Should You Start Considering Marriage?

As a single parent, you need to understand that everything you do has an impact on your children. This means that when you decide to get married again, it isn't just a decision that you can make alone – you need to make sure that your children are ready for the transition as well. Entering into a new relationship as a single parent must be done carefully and slowly – the same goes for entering into a new marriage. You must be absolutely sure that it is what you want and you need to take the time to determine how your children feel about it.

Every situation is different, but marriage is never something you should rush into. But how long should you date your partner before thinking about marriage as an option? If you do some research online you will find recommendations ranging from at least 1 year to a minimum of three years, or more. There is no right or wrong answer – it all depends on your relationship with your partner, how well your children have taken to your partner, and how much the marriage will affect your children.

If your children are already grown and have left the house, remarriage will be less of a challenge than for individuals who have young children. Older children are able to understand that you cannot be expected to live the rest of your life in solitude following a divorce or the death of a spouse. Younger children can have trouble accepting change, however, so you need to tread lightly. You can certainly discuss the option of marriage with your partner but be sure to involve your children in the conversation before you make any decisions.

<u>While there is no formula for determining the right time to start considering remarriage, there are certain things that should happen first, including the following:</u>

- You and your partner should develop a thorough understanding of who the other person is and both of you should fully accept the other for who they are.

- You and your spouse should have talked about your pasts and have had a conversation about what life would be like together.

- You should both have a profound love and respect for one another – physically, mentally, and emotionally.
- Both of your children should have met your partner and have some degree of connection with them.

- You should think carefully and have a conversation with your partner about how your two families will blend.

- You and your partner should discuss the roles each of you will have in the family – talk about how you will share the responsibility of raising your children.

- You should talk with your partner about how you will share the role of disciplining your children.

These are just a few of the many questions the two of you should ask each other when considering remarriage. Depending how your last marriage ended (either by divorce or death), your children could still be feeling the effects of losing a parent. For this reason, you need to be extra sure that remarriage is right for you and your new partner before you bring up with subject with your children.

2.) Tips for Telling Your Children

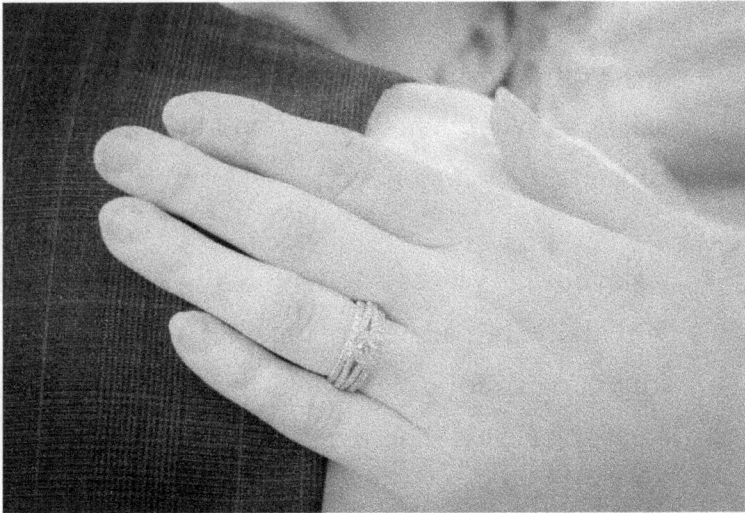

The process of telling your children that you are getting remarried will vary depending on the age of your children and how much exposure they have had to your new partner. The older your children are, the more you will be able to have an open conversation with them. For younger children, it can take time to explain to them what is happening in a way that they can understand. You also need to keep reassuring them that their lives are not going to change and that the new marriage is a good thing. You'll have to use your own discretion regarding when and how to break the news.

Chapter Seven: When Should You Mention the "M" Word?

To help you get through the process of telling your children about your new marriage, here are some tips:

- Ask your kids how they feel about your new partner – ask them what they do and don't like, then address any concerns they may have.

- Ask your kids if they understand what it means that you and your partner are together – it can be difficult for young children to understand why you are seeing someone beside their parent.

- Ask your kids if they would be okay with your partner to start spending more time with the family.

- If your partner has kids, ask your kids how they feel about them and how they would feel if they started spending more time together.

- Ask your kids if they know what it would mean if you and your partner got married – address any concerns or questions they may have about it.

Asking your children these and other questions can help open up an opportunity to talk about your remarriage. As you ask your kids these questions, take their responses to heart and address any questions or concerns they may have. Depending on how your kids respond to these questions, it may be the right time to bring up the issue of remarriage or you may need to table the discussion for later. You should also be prepared for the possibility that one child accepts the idea readily while another does not.

3.) Challenges You Should Expect and How to Deal

When you and your partner are ready to marry, you should expect some challenges as you combine your two families. If your children are older and mostly grown, the transition could be easier than if you have younger children who are having trouble understanding what your new relationship means. The best thing you can do is to be open and honest with your kids – ask them about how they feel about the situation and give them a chance to address any concerns or questions. The worst thing you can do is hide things from your children or assume that they will be okay with you remarrying without actually asking them.

In addition to talking to your kids about getting remarried, you should also talk to them about what it will mean to have a blended family. If your partner has children of their own, you'll need to talk to everyone about what your new blended family situation is going to be like. It is important that your children understand that your new partner is not trying to replace their parent – it can take time for this understanding to develop and, for some children, it never happens at all.

When it comes to remarrying, there are many challenges you will have to face – you and your partner will need to communicate with each other in order to deal with these challenges. Keeping the peace in a blended family can be difficult, especially with step-children involved. Talk to your spouse and your children about who is going to deal out discipline and what role each parent is going to play. Your children should understand that your new spouse is an equal partner, but not a replacement of the other parent. To what degree you allow your partner to discipline your children will depend on how your children feel about your partner and how your partner feels about it.

Creating a healthy, bonded stepfamily is not something that will happen overnight. You and your partner will have to work at it and you will need the cooperation of your children as well. It may help for each of you to spend some time alone with the other's children, assuming that the children are amenable to this idea. You should also make an effort to do things together as a whole family while also spending time alone with your children and your partner with their children.

References

"7 Boring Date Ideas That are Guaranteed to Kill Any Chance of a Relationship." Art of Charm. <http://theartofcharm.com/confidence/7-boring-first-date-ideas-guaranteed-kill-chance-relationship/.

"7 Reasons Why Having Common Interests in a Relationship is Overrated." Gurl.com. <http://www.gurl.com/2015/11/10/reasons-why-having-common-interests-in-a-relationship-is-overrated/>

"10 Steps to Introducing Your New Partner to Your Kids." eHarmony Advice. <http://www.eharmony.com.au/dating-advice/relationships/10-steps-to-introducing-your-new-partner-to-your-kids#.WB-TC5KlwuU>

"15 Reasons to Date a Single Mom." eHarmony. <http://www.eharmony.com/dating-advice/dating-advice-for-you/15-reasons-to-date-a-single-mom/#.WByPeJJhkuU>

"40 Free Date Ideas You'll Both Love." Shape.com. <http://www.shape.com/lifestyle/sex-and-love/40-free-date-ideas-youll-both-love>

Adams, Rebecca. "A Very Good Reason to be Friends Before Dating, Courtesy of Science." The Huffington Post.

<http://www.huffingtonpost.com/2015/07/07/dating-tip-science_n_7736420.html>

Alden, Scott. "Single Parent Dating: 8 Convenient Places to Meet People." Parenting.com. <http://www.parenting.com/gallery/single-parents-dating-guide>

Barker, Eric. "First Date Conversation: 5 Things Research Says You Should Talk About." Time.com. <http://time.com/3087739/first-date-conversation-5-things-research-says-you-should-talk-about/>

Blankenship, Jessica. "9 Reasons Why Single Parents are the Best People to Date." Thought Catalog. <http://thoughtcatalog.com/jessica-blankenship/2014/01/9-reasons-why-single-parents-are-the-best-people-to-date/>

Deal, Ron L. "11 Best Practices for Dating as a Single Parent." Family Life. <http://www.familylife.com/articles/topics/parenting/challenges/single-parenting/11-best-practices-for-dating-as-a-single-parent>

"Finding Time to Date When You're Super Busy." Corporette. <http://corporette.com/finding-time-to-date-when-youre-super-busy/>

"How to Tell the Kids and Your Ex That You're Getting Married Again?" The Huffington Post.

<http://www.huffingtonpost.com/ann-blumenthal-jacobs/how-do-you-tell-the-kids-_b_1130931.html>

"Introducing New Partner Too Fast, Too Soon." Interaction Consultants. <http://www.yoursocialworker.com/s-articles/too_fast_too_soon.pdf>

"Is Remarriage a Step in the Right Direction?" Focus on the Family. <http://www.focusonthefamily.com/lifechallenges/relationship-challenges/blended-families/is-remarriage-the-next-step>

Kim, Jen. "Why Friends First Doesn't Work." Psychology Today. <https://www.psychologytoday.com/blog/valley-girl-brain/201004/why-friends-first-doesnt-work>

LaFata, Alexia. "If You're Friends First, Then You're More Likely to Have a Successful Relationship." Elite Daily. <http://elitedaily.com/life/friends-before-relationship/998876/>

Lifshitz, Laura. "Single Moms: Are You Ready to Introduce Your New Partner to Your Child?" Pop Sugar. <http://www.popsugar.com/moms/Introducing-Your-New-Partner-Your-Child-37800899>

Nicholson, Jeremy. "Pros and Cons of Online Dating." Psychology Today. <https://www.psychologytoday.com/blog/the-attraction-doctor/201404/pros-and-cons-online-dating>

"Science Says Couples in Lasting Relationships Typically Wait This Long to Start Having Sex." Business Insider. <http://www.businessinsider.com/when-should-you-have-sex-in-a-relationship-study-2015-7>

"Single Parents and Sleepovers." Match.com. <http://www.match.com/cp.aspx?cpp=/cppp/magazine/article0.html&articleid=9525>

"Six Simple Secrets of Great Relationships." Centerstone. <https://centerstone.org/health-wellness/links/six-simple-secrets-of-great-relationships>

Smalley, Greg. "Eight Great Reasons to Date." CBN. <http://www1.cbn.com/eight-great-reasons-date>

Solley, Kristen. "10 No-Fail Conversation Starters for a First Date." Women's Health. <http://www.womenshealthmag.com/sex-and-love/first-date-conversation-starters>

Sorohan, Molly. "Ace Your Dinner Date." Match.com. <http://www.match.com/magazine/article/6373/Ace-Your-Dinner-Date/>

"Talking to Your Child About Sex." Healthy Children. <https://www.healthychildren.org/English/ages-stages/gradeschool/puberty/Pages/Talking-to-Your-Child-About-Sex.aspx>

Taylor, Julie. "The Very Best First-Date Moves." Match.com. <http://www.match.com/magazine/article/6790/The-Very-Best-First-Date-Moves/>

"Ten Tips for Those Considering Remarriage." Psychology Today. <https://www.psychologytoday.com/blog/magnetic-partners/201308/ten-tips-those-considering-remarriage>

"What Should I Look For in a Partner?" Love is Respect. <http://www.loveisrespect.org/dating-basics/what-should-i-look-for-in-partner/>

"What Your Child is Experiencing When You Remarry." Healthy Children. <https://www.healthychildren.org/English/family-life/family-dynamics/types-of-families/Pages/What-Your-Child-is-Experiencing-When-You-Remarry.aspx>

Wolf, Jennifer. "Single Parent Statistics." About Parenting. <http://singleparents.about.com/od/legalissues/p/portrait.htm>

Index

D

E

I

J

K

L

M

N

O

P

T

V

W

Feeding Baby
Cynthia Cherry
978-1941070000

Axolotl
Lolly Brown
978-0989658430

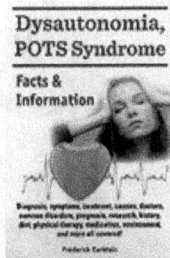

Dysautonomia, POTS
Syndrome
Frederick Earlstein
978-0989658485

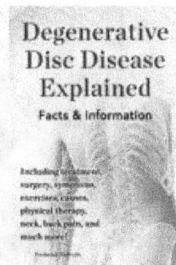

Degenerative Disc
Disease Explained
Frederick Earlstein
978-0989658485

Sinusitis, Hay Fever,
Allergic Rhinitis Explained
Frederick Earlstein
978-1941070024

Wicca
Riley Star
978-1941070130

Zombie Apocalypse
Rex Cutty
978-1941070154

Capybara
Lolly Brown
978-1941070062

Eels As Pets
Lolly Brown
978-1941070167

Scabies and Lice Explained
Frederick Earlstein
978-1941070017

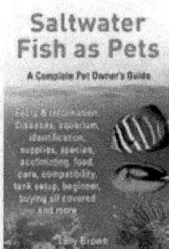

Saltwater Fish As Pets
Lolly Brown
978-0989658461

Torticollis Explained
Frederick Earlstein
978-1941070055

Kennel Cough
Lolly Brown
978-0989658409

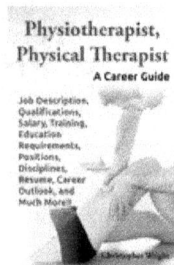

Physiotherapist, Physical
Therapist
Christopher Wright
978-0989658492

Rats, Mice, and Dormice
As Pets
Lolly Brown
978-1941070079

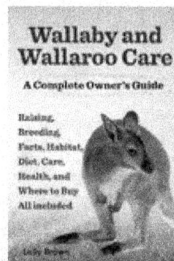

Wallaby and Wallaroo Care
Lolly Brown
978-1941070031

Bodybuilding Supplements
Explained
Jon Shelton
978-1941070239

Demonology
Riley Star
978-19401070314

Pigeon Racing
Lolly Brown
978-1941070307

Dwarf Hamster
Lolly Brown
978-1941070390

Cryptozoology
Rex Cutty
978-1941070406

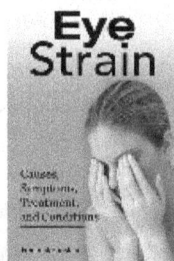

Eye Strain
Frederick Earlstein
978-1941070369

Inez The Miniature Elephant
Asher Ray
978-1941070353

Vampire Apocalypse
Rex Cutty
978-1941070321

www.ingramcontent.com/pod-product-compliance
Lightning Source LLC
Chambersburg PA
CBHW050549280326
41933CB00011B/1777